Shakes, Sodas, & Smoothies

Shakes, Sodas, & Smoothies

Deborah Gray

AN IMPRINT OF RUNNING PRESS
PHILADELPHIA • LONDON

Dedication

For Atherton and Jo, who gallantly tested
recipes even on the coldest of days.

A QUINTET BOOK

ISBN 0-7624-0196-6

Library of Congress
Cataloging-in-Publication Number 97-68289

This book was designed and produced by
Quintet Publishing Limited
The Old Brewery
6 Blundell Street
London N7 9BH

Creative Director: Richard Dewing
Art Director: Clare Reynolds
Designer: Fiona Roberts @ The Design Revolution
Project Editor: Clare Hubbard
Editor: Jane Donovan
Food Stylist: Jennie Berresford
Photographer: Philip Wilkins
Picture on page 16: Waring Products DN Dynamics Corp. of America

Typeset in Great Britain by
Central Southern Typesetters, Eastbourne
Manufactured in Singapore by Bright Arts Pte Ltd.
Printed in China by Leefung-Asco Printers Ltd.

Courage Books, an imprint of
Running Press Book Publishers
125 South Twenty-second Street
Philadelphia, Pennsylvania 19103-4399

Because of the risk of salmonella poisoning, raw
eggs should not be served to the very young,
the ill or elderly, or to pregnant women.

Contents

The Rise of the Shake & Soda

The history of milk shakes and sodas is linked not only with that of ice cream, but also with the history of transportation, industrialization, emigration, prohibition, economics, and war. Our story begins in the seventeenth century when ice creams were first enjoyed by the wealthy and remained the preserve of the rich for the next two centuries. Then, in the middle of the nineteenth century, the trade in the storage of ice in ice houses took off and improved transportation made ice much more widely available throughout Europe and America, even in towns as far south as Miami. At the same time, unrest during the unification of Italy drove young Italians abroad in search of a new life. Thousands of emigrants settled in America as well as in many other northern European countries. They brought with them their love of *gelato* (ice cream) and, with the ice now in place, they set up as ice cream makers and street vendors, from Philadelphia to Glasgow.

In England, in 1843, a machine for the freezing and churning of ice creams on a commercial scale was invented. Three years later an American housewife invented the domestic machine for churning by hand and this has changed little in design to this day.

The 145-year-old White Mountain Co.'s hand-driven ice-cream maker. Its design is little changed from early days.

It was at this stage that America took up the whole idea of ice cream and ran with it. Until this time ice creams had been made largely on a small scale and sold in confectionery stores, with prices controlled by cartel. In 1851 Jacob Fussell Jr., a Baltimore milk dealer, found that he could make more money by manufacturing ice cream from his milk. He broke down the cartels and sold ice cream at a price that was less than half of that of his rivals. Others followed suit and soon ice cream was widely available and extremely fashionable. Around the same time, advances in continuous freeze technology, along with the development of condensed and dried milks, made the mass production of ice creams much more feasible.

During this period the first soda fountains were being established. These were originally found only in drug stores as the druggist was the only person in town who knew how to correctly handle the gases and acids that were required in the production of carbonated water. It was discovered that a mixture of carbonic gas in water is unstable and causes gases to rise in the liquid on exposure to air. As long as the bubbling goes on, the temperature of the water is reduced, resulting in a drink with a brisk, refreshing taste. Soda water was then made by adding a little bicarbonate of soda to the water before carbonation and seltzer was achieved by adding mineral salts. The druggist also produced sweet mineral waters that were flavored with syrups.

These novel drinks were particularly appealing during the long, hot summers. The process was not perfect, however, and explosions in drug stores were a fairly common event. In spite of this, soda fountains soon became popular meeting places, characterized by a light atmosphere. This advice was given to soda fountain owners:

> *It is practically impossible to approach the modern soda fountain, except in a happy mood. Candy is happy eating for happy people and you can say the same thing for soda fountain refreshment. People who are harassed or sad do not select a soda fountain unless they want cheering ... Make your soda fountain service sparkle with good will and cordiality.*

J. O. Dahl, 1930

The early bars were characterized by rows of jars holding the sweet, colorful syrups and a carbonator which had a draft arm to draw up the carbonated water. Later, with the advent of refrigeration, an ice box was added and later still, the bottles of syrup were incorporated into a box-like structure that stood on the counter or was hung onto the wall. Once refrigeration was introduced and technology had improved, the way was clear to bring ice cream to the soda fountain. Ice cream soon became a central feature, if not the main focus of the fountain. Soda fountains were then at the height of their popularity and the owners could afford to spend money on decorations and on creating the happy atmosphere that was evidently sought after by their customers. The delights of these stylish art deco soda fountains were captured by the early movies and in popular advertisements which have remained implanted in most people's visual memory.

Early soda fountains provided drinks made from fruit juice in place of the chemical concoctions offered by makers of bottled mineral waters. Juices and syrups were often made on site or purchased from manufacturers who could ensure uniform quality and taste. By 1930 a range of over 30 different syrups was available from one manufacturer alone. To compete with the cola manufacturers' high profile marketing and advertising techniques, soda fountains were offering handouts, coupons, and other enticements to encourage people to drink fountain sodas.

In the mid-nineteenth century the prohibition movement began to gather force in an attempt to end alcohol abuse and related sins. The soda fountain became the best friend of the prohibitionists and, even before the introduction of the prohibition laws in January 1920, financial interests united behind the soda fountain which saw a rapid expansion in numbers throughout the 1920s. By 1930 there were over 100,000 soda fountains in the United States. The soda fountain became a community center where shakes and sodas could be enjoyed at leisure. They were installed in diners, new hotels, department stores, gas stations, in parks, airports, and

This sign is the centerpiece of the five-piece "Nasturtium" festoon, which would have been used to decorate the backbar of a soda fountain (1929).

Introduction

even in large apartment blocks. It seemed that every town, however remote, had its own soda fountain. Then, in December 1933, came the repeal of prohibition laws—the heyday of the soda fountain was over.

Soda fountains as such never recovered from their decline in the mid 1930s, but strict drinking laws maintained the popularity of the ice cream parlor especially in the years immediately following World War II. Today, ice cream parlors are no longer thought of as the social center that they once were. However, it isn't necessary to visit an ice cream parlor to enjoy a shake, they can be found at locations from trendy restaurants, department stores, to drinks stands in theme parks, they can even be purchased ready made in the market.

In the 1980s, prosperity led to the expansion in gourmet ice creams for sale both in the market and in stylish new ice cream stores. These high-quality ices, based on real fruit and quality chocolate, breathed new life into the shake and soda business too. Wonderful, rich ice cream shakes full of extraordinary goodies were introduced, spurred on by a competitive drive to be the best.

At the same time, an increased awareness of the peril of a high fat diet increased the interest in sorbets and fruit-based sodas. This awareness drove the introduction of frozen yogurt, which has retained its separate identity from ice cream and there are now outlets producing refreshing drinks using frozen yogurt. The latest player in the soft drinks field is the coffee bar, selling a wide variety of quality iced coffees and coffee-based shakes.

Most of the drinks featured in this book owe their origins to the soda fountain. We no longer have to shave ice from a large block using a plane and our huge variety of ice creams can be easily stored in a domestic freezer, but the principles are largely the same. Some tastes have changed, crème de caçoa is now preferred to crème de menthe and most of us would prefer to balance the sweetness of our drinks with lemon or lime juice in preference to acid phosphate. However, our great-grandparents would recognize many of the delicious range of shakes, sodas, and coolers found in the following chapters. Our approach hasn't changed much either, we still look upon shakes and sodas as happy drinking.

Ingredients

The quality of the shakes and sodas that you make depends on the quality of the ingredients that go into them. Bear this in mind, but these are essentially fun foods that should be quick to make from items that are readily available.

Nutritionally, some of the shakes in this book should be regarded as an occasional treat. There are plenty of lower-fat drinks which are every bit as indulgent. To some extent the sugar content of the drinks is at your discretion although most iced products are high in sugar or sugar substitutes. It has to be admitted that there is minimal fiber in a chocolate shake but there is more in a shake made with whole fruits such as bananas—you could even fortify your shake with wheat germ. There is a wide range of reduced fat and low-calorie products on the market so even those on restricted diets can enjoy a variety of delicious shakes. The following information may help you to choose wisely when shopping for flavorful ingredients.

Ice Cream

We all think that we know what ice cream is. On closer inspection, it is amazing to discover what a complex chemical substance we are dealing with. The characteristic taste, texture, and density come from a delicate balance of water, sugar, air, and butterfat plus flavoring. Creaminess depends on the amount of butterfat solids in the ice cream. This must be ten percent in most ice creams dropping to eight percent in fruity or nutty ones. At the gourmet end of the market the fat content may be as much as 18 percent. French-style ice cream, based on a custard, also contains eggs. The higher the fat content, the denser the ice cream and the smoother the texture. These rich ice creams make good, creamy, thick shakes.

Reduced fat or 'light' ice creams contain under ten percent fat solids. These are made using powdered milk, evaporated, and condensed milks which contain less fat than whole milk and cream. To further increase their lightness, they are whipped to incorporate more air than true ice creams and often use artificial sweeteners and a variety of stabilizers and emulsifiers. These products are all different. They will make reasonably good shakes but are less creamy, and the resulting shakes will be thinner than their higher-fat cousins. Experiment with different brands to find the one that most suits your taste.

With the huge variety of ice creams on the market there must be a good reason for the revival in home-made. Home-made ice cream has a deliciously fresh flavor that can be tailored to individual taste and you know exactly what ingredients have been used. It is also inexpensive when compared to store-bought ice cream of similar quality. In addition, contemporary ice cream-making machines are easy to use and produce consistently good textured ice creams. (For recipes, see pages 20–21.)

Whatever type of ice cream you choose, you will find that strong flavors work best in shakes where the flavors are diluted down with additional milk, fruit juice, or water. Do be careful to avoid ice creams that use a lot of synthetic flavoring or your shakes may have a chemical aftertaste. The ice creams used in this book have been restricted to the most popular flavors with the widest availability. It is hoped that many of the ideas will act as a springboard for your own ideas and you will go on to create fantastic shakes using more esoteric flavors. Similarly exploit the vast array of textured ice creams packed with candies and cookies, nuts, and fruits.

Frozen Yogurt

Frozen yogurt has become extremely popular and is now a serious rival to ice cream. It is similar in texture to the soft-serve ice creams, with a slightly sharp underlying taste. Again, frozen yogurt comes in whole fat, reduced, and non-fat varieties. Whole fat frozen yogurt tends to be based on Russian-style yogurts and contains around ten percent fat. When lower-fat yogurts are used, stabilizers and emulsifiers have to be added to prevent the mixture from forming large ice crystals. In addition, most of the beneficial bacteria in yogurt are destroyed by the freezing process thus reducing its nutritional benefits over ice cream.

Despite the fact that frozen yogurt may not be quite as healthy as it first appears, many yogurts are absolutely delicious and form the basis for smoothies. Frozen yogurt can be successfully made at home using either commercial yogurts or those made from scratch (see page 46). As they are not dependent on custards or the incorporation of eggs and cream, they are simpler and quicker to prepare than most ice creams.

Sherbets

The word 'sherbet' originally came from the Middle East where it was used to describe a cold, sweetened fruit drink but the term has been used to describe all manner of iced preparations throughout the ages. Today it usually refers to frozen, sweetened fruit juices, to which a little milk is added—resulting in a fat content of around two percent. Recently, non-fruit flavors have also been introduced and make good iced drinks. However, sherbets may be considerably lower in fat than ice creams but they do have more sugar. Sherbets also contain a small amount of citric acid which occurs naturally in citrus fruit and gives them their characteristic tangy taste.

Made from sherbets, coolers are marvelous, thirst-quenching summer drinks. They have a hint of creaminess and a tinge of sharpness, plus the full

unmasked flavor of the fruit. Sherbets are sometimes difficult to purchase, but they are easy and very inexpensive to make at home (see page 51).

Sorbet or Water Ice

These are similar to sherbets but are made solely with water and are often of a softer consistency. Sorbets often contain alcohol and form the basis for some excellent refreshing coolers and sodas for adults. However, home-made sorbets often contain raw egg whites and these should be avoided if you are pregnant or have a weak immune system.

Coolers, floats, cocktails, and iced punches made from sorbets are wonderfully refreshing—perfect for a summer party.

Soy Ice Cream

Good soy ice cream is a fairly new commodity and the best varieties have a taste that is very similar to real ice cream although some have a flavor more like a cross between frozen yogurt and ice cream with a slightly beany, nutty taste. Often referred to as a frozen dessert, soy ice cream is a non-dairy, low-fat product that can be substituted in most recipes and used in combination with milk or soy milk. Some of these products are surprisingly good and are well worth investigating particularly by those on restricted diets or parents who are trying to keep tabs on their children's unhealthy tastes. Substitute soy ice cream in any recipe that calls for ice cream. The end result will be less rich and frothy than if gourmet ice cream were used, but it will also be a much healthier drink.

Storing Ice Cream

Home-made ice cream should be eaten as soon as possible. It should be kept in a clean, plastic, air-tight container in the freezer for no more than two weeks if it is to retain its flavor; four weeks for sorbets. The longer the ice cream is stored, the more the flavor will

deteriorate and the texture will become increasingly icy. This advice applies to purchased ice creams and sorbets as well as to home-produced. Never store ice cream beyond the recommended period as detailed on the packaging and never refreeze ice cream that has melted.

Milk

Whole milk produces the traditional, rich, thick shake but good shakes can be made from lowfat milk and from skim milk. Of course the lower-fat shake will be more watery but provided you use good-quality, strong flavors this is not necessarily detrimental. In fact, so many people have been weaned off the taste of butterfats that some most definitely prefer the latter. However, it is the high butterfat content of whole milk that holds the bubbles and makes shakes so frothy. It is mainly for this reason that whole milk is recommended throughout this book. If you are using dried milk powder, try to reconstitute it two hours before use to allow the flavor to develop.

Buttermilk and soy milk can be substituted for milk in most of the recipes. However, soy milk works best with banana, coffee, nutty, and carob flavors which blend well with its beany taste. It is also good combined with malts. Soy milk with chocolate is disappointing and the subtlety of vanilla is lost when combined with soy milk. Buttermilk has a slightly acidic quality that works particularly well with sherbets. Omit any lemon or lime juice in a recipe if you are substituting buttermilk as its own sharpness will probably be sufficient.

Syrups

Recently, there has been an explosion of taste in the world of syrups and a vast and somewhat eccentric range of flavors can be found. Sophisticated amaretto or macadamia nut, tempting Irish Cream, sun-kissed guava, and even pumpkin pie flavored syrups are available to try. The opportunity for inventive milk shakes is therefore unlimited. Use syrups with a light hand an

Introduction

balance the sweetness with a little lemon or lime juice as they did in the old days. If you are making ice cream at home using syrups, consider reducing the sugar content of your ice cream by about one-third.

There is also a reasonable range of sugar-free syrups which can be combined with 'light' ice creams, frozen yogurts, and sorbets to make guilt-free gourmet shakes and sodas for those on restrictive diets. Be aware that these syrups are every bit as sweet as those which use sugar and must be used with the same caution. In addition to using syrup to flavor milk shakes, it also makes a good topping to drizzle into the shake or soda in a concentrated rivulet of taste. For instance, a strong vein of peppermint is excellent in a chocolate shake, or a trickle of strawberry is a sweet treat in a tart lemon sherbet-based cooler, and a coffee shake could be topped with whipped cream drizzled with cinnamon syrup.

Simple sugar syrups are the simplest way to sweeten shakes and sodas as the liquid sugar easily mixes with the liquid and does not sink to the bottom in a sweet mass. Simply dissolve one cup of sugar in one cup of boiling water, cool, and place in a sterilized sealed bottle.

Vanilla or *Cinnamon Syrup*
MAKES 4 CUPS

2 cups mineral water, boiled
2 cups sugar
1 vanilla bean or cinnamon stick

Pour the boiling water over the sugar, then stir until dissolved. Add a vanilla bean or cinnamon stick to the hot syrup. Let cool. Leave the spices in the syrup while storing.

Strawberry *Syrup*
MAKES 1¾ CUPS

1½ lb. strawberries
Sugar (see method)
Juice of 1 lemon

Hull the strawberries and purée in a food processor. Line a non-metallic sieve with a double layer of cheesecloth. Strain the purée, then lightly squeeze to extract as much juice as possible. Measure the juice into a saucepan and add 1¼ cups of sugar for every cup of juice. Cook over a low heat until all the syrup has dissolved. Stir in the lemon juice, cool for 5 minutes, then place in a sterilized jar.

Fruit

Most fruits (in purée form or juiced) can be used alone or in fabulous combinations in almost all types of shakes and sodas. It is best to use very ripe fruit as a basis for shakes and sodas, preferably those ripened on the vine rather than fruits picked green and ripened on the store shelf. Peel the skin away from any thick-skinned fruit or wash thoroughly. You can purée the fruit immediately but to release the juices and get the very best out of it, chop into chunks and sprinkle over a little sugar, cover, and leave for a couple of hours. Then purée in a food processor or mash with a potato masher. It is a matter of personal preference whether or not seeded fruit such as raspberries are passed through a non-metallic sieve to remove the seeds.

Some varieties of fruit work better if they are gently cooked before use particularly if the fruit is not very ripe. Plums, apricots, cherries, and blueberries, for instance, develop a richness in their cooked form that is different from their uncooked, sparkling fresh taste. Cook over low heat using the minimum amount of water and sugar until just soft. Cool and purée. Remember to reduce the corresponding quantity of sugar when making up the drink.

Apples and similar fruits are better juiced than puréed. Juices can be made at home using a juicer or purchased. There are now fabulous, exotic juice combinations in the grocery stores and even more tempting choices in health food outlets. All you need is a bottle of juice, a couple of scoops of sorbet, and blend all the ingredients together with a blender to produce a real taste sensation.

Frozen fruits can be used as fresh fruit or they may be used as the basis of an iced drink that contains no ice cream or sorbet. Canned and bottled fruit are also good standbys. Purée these down with their juices and treat like a syrup. Fruit preserves can also be substituted for a syrup with the addition of a little water.

Alcohol

If you are making your own ice cream and sorbets you should be aware that alcohol depresses the freezing temperature and may prevent your ice cream from freezing. It is best to follow a recipe carefully and not to be enthusiastically over-generous! By the same token, alcohol should be added to the shake at the last minute as it causes the ice crystals to melt more quickly.

Chocolate

It is simplest to use chocolate ice cream, chocolate syrups, or chocolate milk when making shakes. You can use cocoa powder and chocolate drink powder but mix with milk or water first following the manufacturer's instructions. However, use a minimum quantity of hot liquid to dissolve the powder and top up with cold. If you are using melted chocolate, this must be combined with milk or cream while it is still warm or it will re-solidify too quickly when in contact with the cold ice cream, making the shake bitty. Chocolate chips and chunks, of course, can be added liberally.

Coffee

For a well-flavored coffee shake, use espresso coffee as your base as it has sufficient taste not to be overwhelmed by the addition of milk or ice cream and its bitterness is well balanced by the sweetness of the added sugar. Alternatively, use any good coffee and experiment with the variety of flavored coffees that are now available. Orange coffee, tiramisu, and spiced coffees all make excellent bases for a coffee shake. Be aware that there is a risk of making over-sweet coffee shakes if you are relying entirely on coffee syrup for flavoring. The combined sweetness of the syrup and the ice cream may result in the loss of the characteristic bitterness craved by coffee lovers.

Vanilla

Vanilla has a deliciously, aromatic flavor. The subtlest way to impart the flavor of the vanilla bean is to allow it to infuse in hot milk for 15 minutes. Let cool and chill before using in shakes. Alternatively, use vanilla extract. Avoid synthetic 'flavoring'—look for products made from the best-quality beans, if possible. The best vanilla beans are thought to be from Madagascar, Mexico, and Tahiti. You can make your own vanilla sugar which has a fine, subtle flavor. Simply place a bean in 2 cups of granulated sugar and seal in a jar. Leave for about a week and it is ready to use. Beans used in an infusion can be reused to make sugar.

Malt

This can be added to the shake in powdered form and added to the mixture in the blender, or malted milk may be added. Either way, malt adds the richness of barley to the shake and produces some of the best shakes of all times. The flavor of the malt works particularly well with vanilla and chocolate ice cream.

Toppings

When choosing a topping, select a color, texture, and flavor that provides contrast yet complements the flavor of the shake. The chocolate on top of the Key Lime Shake (see page 25) is a good example of this or use sliced Brazil nuts on top of an exotic fruit shake.

Traditionalists may wish to simply add a swirl of whipped cream (not synthetic!) or a scoop of ice cream and a drizzle of syrup—or a shake of powdered chocolate, cinnamon or nutmeg. Others may be tempted by candies such as chocolate or peanut butter chips; better still, take a good-quality bittersweet chocolate bar or chocolate-covered after dinner mints and cut into chunks. Chocolate and colored sprinkles and mini marshmallows are always popular too. Keep an eye open for unusual candies, e.g. chocolate-coated flakes (a recent find) are really excellent and chocolate-coated coffee beans make a perfect sophisticated garnish. Similarly, experiment with crushed cookies—Italian amaretti are excellent and crushed health bars work well too.

How To ...

Get the full flavor from citrus fruits

1 To make citrus fruit easier to juice, warm the fruit slightly by placing in a bowl of hot water.

2 Wash the fruit and using a small, sharp knife, pare off the zest to leave the white pith. Long shreds of zest can be placed in cold water to form curls for decorating.

3 Cut each fruit in half; place one half at a time in the squeezer with the cut surface facing downwards. Squeeze and strain juice.

Crush ice to a fine snow

1 Lay a clean cloth on a work surface. Spread ice cubes over one half of the cloth; fold the other over to cover the ice. Use a mallet to crush the ice, striking firmly and, for finely crushed ice, repeatedly.

2 Unfold the cloth and, with a spoon or ice shovel, scrape the crushed ice lightly away from the cloth. Transfer to a jug or directly into glasses.

Make a purée from fibrous fruit

1 To prepare pineapples or any other fibrous fruit, first cut the top off the fruit. Holding the fruit upright with one hand, slice the skin off in strips, turning the fruit round as you cut it. Cut the flesh into 1-inch chunks.

2 Put the chunks of fruit into a food processor or a blender. Process until evenly and smoothly puréed. For a really smooth texture, pass through a sieve.

Fresh fruit can be added in purée form or in small chunks. Some exotic fruits such as passion fruit and granadilla lend themselves particularly well to toppings as their flesh can simply be scooped out and drizzled over the froth. Peel or skin from citrus fruit can be cut into decorative shapes using cookie cutters. All types of nuts or toasted coconut can be used and some breakfast cereals, such as grape nuts, make good crunchy toppings.

Toppings do not have to remain on top of the shake—they can be stirred in. A luxurious cappuccino shake with chocolate chips is particularly successful, as are smooth fresh fruit shakes with chunky fresh fruit additions. If you do decide to stir in your topping, remember that cookies and breakfast cereals become soggy when they make contact with liquid so these shakes should not be left for too long.

Equipment

Equipment for Shakes

Ice cream parlors have specially-designed shake making machines but for home use the essential piece of equipment for making shakes and sodas is the blender. There are a number of options on the market but without a doubt, the best is the stand-alone, professional blender. The blenders available today are based on designs from the 1930s. Not only do they look fabulous, but they have a large 2 pint capacity and their weight gives them stability in use. They usually have around a 450-watt motor and at least a dual speed option. The higher power that these machines provide is necessary if you want to make smooth coolers and other drinks that involve crushing ice. In just a few seconds they will do the job perfectly.

The blender attachment on a food processor is fine for making most shakes, but add ice and it will simply vanish in the processing, serving just to water down your drink. If you have a hand-held blender, you will find this adequate for most drinks although be sure to blend in a deep and narrow container to prevent splashing. Again, this will not crush ice. Failing all else, you can use a cocktail shaker and elbow grease!

You will find that a strong ice cream scoop, a good knife, a chopping board, and a mallet for crushing ice are also handy.

Ice Cream Makers

Serious ice cream and shake makers may choose to make their own ice cream. For this, an ice cream-making machine is necessary. Recipe books may tell you that you can break down ice crystals by beating them with a fork: you can't. It is highly unlikely that you will achieve a really smooth and satisfactory ice cream. A small ice cream maker churns and freezes the mixture simultaneously and makes the most delicious ice cream. The only disadvantage is that you need to be well prepared in order to use some machines as the bowl must be placed in the freezer for around 8 hours prior to use. This is unnecessary with the more expensive models.

You will also need a heatproof bowl, a wooden spoon, an electric mixer or balloon whisk, a saucepan, and a heat diffuser. The heat diffuser is particularly important as it is very easy to overcook the custard when making ice cream. A diffuser reduces the heat under the pan and reduces the risk of curdling.

Syrup-making

Home-made syrup is often best. You will require a two-pint heatproof jug, a small, heavy saucepan, and a wooden spoon to reach into the bottom edge of the pan, where sugary substances always seem to burn. For making caramel or toffee sauces, a sugar thermometer may also be useful.

Presentation

Glasses

You can have a lot of fun when presenting your shakes and sodas. The range of glassware available is staggering and stylish plastic glasses are easy to find. Generally, glasses should have a capacity of between one and two cups except those for cocktail shakes which look excellent when served in the appropriate cocktail glass. Be careful when using colored glasses; think about the color of the shake and choose a complementary glass— a chocolate shake in a green glass looks less than appealing. Also avoid thin, delicate glasses which are easily broken and chipped, and may not appreciate extremes of temperature.

Each delicous recipe makes
enough for 1 large or
two small drinks unless
otherwise stated.

Place glasses in the freezer before use. This gives them a lovely frosted appearance and keeps the shakes cold. You can also decorate the rim of the glass by dipping in a little beaten egg white or syrup, then press the rim gently into sugar or chocolate sprinkles.

Keep an eye open for accessories such as cocktail sticks, long-handled spoons, wide straws, cocktail umbrellas, and paper fruits.

Garnishes

An imaginative garnish can transform an ordinary shake into a visual sensation. Use whipped cream, scoops of ice cream or sherbet dripping in hot fudge sauce, blueberry or maple syrup. Top with shaved chocolate, ground cinnamon or nutmeg, curls of citrus zest, piles of berries, slices of fresh or preserved fruit, toasted nuts, and children's candies or add a few sophisticated chocolate-coated coffee beans. Be cool and healthy or outrageously wicked.

Shakes, Sodas, & Smoothies

Shakes rich, smooth, satisfying,

tempting Smoothies and Coolers

clean, fresh, sparkling, flavorful

Sodas lively, tangy, luscious, elegant.

Shakes

The best shakes are made from good ice cream. Blend with milk, fruit, chocolate, or coffee, and some milk and, hey presto, the perfect shake. Choose a really rich, strongly-flavored ice cream which uses real vanilla in preference to one with vanilla flavoring. Look out for those using Bourbon vanilla from Madagascar which produces a particularly full-flavored ice cream. Better still, make your own ice cream.

Ice Cream

Check the manufacturer's instructions before using your ice-cream machine to ensure that it is suitable for use with these recipes. The first recipe is very quick and easy as it requires no cooking. However, it does use raw eggs (see note page 4) so it is unsuitable for the very young or old, pregnant women, and others with a compromised immune system. Alternatively, use a pasteurized dried egg powder, made up according to the manufacturer's instructions. French Vanilla Ice Cream is based on a custard, where the eggs are cooked. Both recipes adapt themselves well to flavoring. Allow ice cream to rest for 15 minutes in the refrigerator before using to make shakes.

Quick Vanilla *Ice Cream*

This recipe is simple to make and is delicious used in shakes and tastes heavenly. Vanilla has a wonderful aromatic flavor, be sure to use a good quality extract.

MAKES 2 PINTS
3 eggs (see note, page 4)
½ cup plus 2 Tbsp. sugar
2 cups heavy or whipping cream, chilled
1 cup whole milk, chilled
2 tsp. good vanilla extract

Whisk the eggs until light and fluffy, about 2 minutes using an electric mixer. Slowly add the sugar and continue to whisk for another minute. Stir in the cream, milk, and vanilla, and chill for 30 minutes.

Place in the ice-cream machine and process following the manufacturer's instructions, usually 20 to 30 minutes. Transfer to a plastic box and freeze to firm.

French Vanilla *Ice Cream*

Based on a traditional French recipe, this ice cream is simply wonderful.

MAKES 1½ PINTS
3 egg yolks
½ cup sugar
1 cup whole milk
¾ cup heavy or whipping
   cream, chilled
1½ tsp. vanilla extract

Beat the egg yolks and the sugar together in a bowl until thick and pale, about 2 minutes using an electric mixer. Bring the milk to a boil and pour over the egg mixture beating continuously. Return the mixture to a pan and place on a heat diffuser over a low heat. (This is important as it is very easy to overheat and curdle the custard if cooked over direct heat.) Stir with a wooden spoon until the mixture is thick enough to coat the back of a spoon. To cook in the microwave, leave in the bowl and cook on low for 10 to 15 minutes stirring every minute until thickened.

Place a circle of damp waxed paper over the surface to prevent a skin from forming and cool; then chill. Fold in the cream and vanilla and continue as for Quick Vanilla.

Strawberry Ice Cream:
1 quantity of either of the vanilla ice creams. Reduce vanilla to 1 teaspoon and add 1 pint mashed strawberries before adding the cream.

Chocolate Ice Cream:
1 quantity of either of the vanilla ice cream recipes. Reduce vanilla to 1 teaspoon and increase sugar to 1 cup. Melt two 2 ounce squares semisweet chocolate and add to the mixture before chilling.

Coffee Ice Cream:
Omit the vanilla and add 3 tablespoons good quality instant coffee before chilling, or stir in ½ cup strong espresso coffee.

Vanilla Shakes

This family of milk shakes contains some old friends including Classic Banana Shake and Key Lime. Other fruit shakes take advantage of the widespread availability of tropical fruits, such as mangoes and cantaloupes, which work wonderfully well alone or in exotic combinations. Experiment with different flavors yourself. The fruit should be really ripe to make the most of all the natural juices and sugars. Don't forget to use whole milk as this has sufficient fat to make a creamy, frothy shake. Shakes made from reduced fat milk will not have the same bubbly texture and richness of flavor. Do not over-blend the shakes or they will become thin.

Plain
Vanilla Shake

Serve this shake in its basic form or use with a variety of different toppings, stirred into the ice cream for flavor and interest.

1 cup whole milk
2 scoops vanilla ice cream
Grated good quality chocolate or nutmeg, to decorate

Place the milk and vanilla ice cream in a blender and process until smooth and frothy. Serve in a tall glass over ice. Garnish with grated chocolate or nutmeg.

> ### Tip
> Make your ice cubes from milk to reduce the diluting effect of water.

Magnificent *Mango*

A basic recipe that can be adapted to suit most fruits.

½ ripe mango
2 scoops vanilla ice cream
¾ cup whole milk
1 tsp. lime juice
Passion fruit pulp, to decorate

Peel the mango, cut the flesh from the pit, and place in the blender. Process until smooth. Add the ice cream, milk, and lime juice and blend for 30 seconds. Pour into the glass and garnish with the fruit pulp. Alternatively, stir the pulp into the mixture for a textured shake.

Variations
Omit the mango and lime juice and make the following substitutions:

Peachy Shake: 1 ripe peach, peeled and pitted.

Berry Shake: Use ½ cup of hulled strawberries, raspberries, or blueberries; or a combination of berries. For a really smooth shake, press the berries through a non-metallic strainer.

Left: **Classic Banana Shake**

Tip

The combination of rich vanilla ice cream and fresh fruit produces a shake that is sweet enough for most palates. Should you require a sweeter shake, add up to 1 tablespoon sugar syrup, sugar, or honey. Don't forget: the riper the fruit, the sweeter the flavor.

Classic *Banana Shake*

The oldest shake in the book.

1 small ripe banana
1 cup whole milk
2 scoops vanilla ice cream
1 tsp. sugar (optional)
1 tsp. lemon juice (optional)
Grated nutmeg, banana slices, to decorate

Peel and chop the banana into chunks. Place in the blender along with the milk, ice cream, sugar, and lemon juice. Process for 30 seconds until smooth. Pour into glasses and decorate with grated nutmeg and banana slices.

Variations

Banoffee Shake: Use toffee or fudge flavored ice cream, top with whipped cream, and grated chocolate.

Maple Banana: Use maple syrup flavored ice cream. Add a scoop of ice cream and drizzle maple syrup over top.

Shakes

Fruit *Combo*

Choose complementary flavors and good quality ripe fruit to make a perfect shake every time. For a really smooth shake, purée the fruit in the blender, then press through a non-metallic strainer.

2 scoops vanilla ice cream
½ cup whole milk
½ cup diced ripe cantaloupe
¼ cup raspberries
Sugar syrup (optional)
4 to 5 raspberries, mint leaves, and melon slice, to decorate

Place the ice cream, milk, cantaloupe, and raspberries in a blender and process until smooth. Taste and sweeten, if desired. Pour into the glass and top with a few additional raspberries, mint leaves, and a melon slice.

Variation
Omit the cantaloupe and raspberries and make the following substitution:

Kiwi & Strawberry Shake: Use 1 diced ripe kiwi fruit and ¼ cup hulled strawberries with 1 tablespoon lime juice.

Tip
The addition of lemon or lime juice often brings out the flavor of the fruit. Adjust to suit your own taste.

Key *Lime*

This shake is refreshing and has a pleasant tartness which offsets the sweetness of the ice cream and chocolate. This shake fits into a regular tumbler-sized glass.

½ **lemon**
½ **lime**
1½ **to 2 Tbsp. sugar**
1 **cup whole milk**
2 **scoops vanilla ice cream**
3 **Tbsp. semisweet chocolate chips or sprinkles**
Whipped cream (optional)
Semisweet chocolate chips or sprinkles and citrus peel curls, to decorate

Wash the lemon and lime well and cut into pieces. Place in the blender with the sugar and milk and process until only tiny flecks of skin are visible. Sift through a non-metallic strainer, pressing out all the liquid.

Return to the blender and add the ice cream. Process until smooth. Pour and stir in the chocolate chips or sprinkles. Top with whipped cream, if using, and decorate with chocolate chips or sprinkles and citrus peel curls. For a smoother shake, simply omit the chocolate chips or sprinkles.

Shakes

Flavored Ice Cream Shakes

The simplest way to make a flavored milk shake is to combine flavored ice cream and milk. The number of different flavors available on the market is astonishing and the range in ice cream parlors is amazing! If you make your own ice cream then the choice of flavors is infinite and limited only by the capacity of the freezer.

Double
Fudge Treat

The fudge ice cream and topping is too good to be true. Avoid hot fudge sauce as it warms up the shake too quickly and can make it sickly.

1 cup whole milk
3 scoops fudge chunk or toffee
   ripple ice cream
¼ cup fudge sauce
1 Tbsp. chopped roasted
   almonds

Place the milk and 2 scoops of ice cream in the blender and process until just smooth. Avoid over-blending, particularly if you are using the textured fudge chunk ice cream, otherwise the chunks will be blended into the shake. Pour the shake into a chilled glass and top with the additional scoop of ice cream. Drizzle over the fudge sauce and sprinkle with nuts.

Coconut Hula *Scream*

The delicious flavor of coconut is satisfying and refreshing.

1 cup cold whole milk
2 scoops coconut ice cream
Pineapple wedge, to decorate

Simply place the milk and ice cream in the blender and process until smooth and frothy. Serve over ice, decorated with a fresh pineapple wedge.

Variation
Coconut Chip: Stir in 2 tablespoons semisweet chocolate chips after blending and top with chocolate shavings.

Marshmallow *Foam*

This shake will remind you of summer camp—especially if you serve it with a toasted marshmallow.

1 cup whole milk
¼ cup mini marshmallows
2 scoops raspberry ice cream
Mini marshmallows or one large toasted marshmallow, to decorate

Heat the milk and the marshmallows until the marshmallows are beginning to melt. Let chill in the refrigerator. Place in a blender with the raspberry ice cream and process until smooth and very foamy. Pour into a glass and serve decorated with a few mini marshmallows or 1 large toasted marshmallow on a toothpick.

Left: **Marshmallow Foam**

Shakes

Malties

Using malted milk gives the shake
extra density of taste and this works
best with simple flavors. Malt comes
from barley which is just sprouting
when it is milled so capturing both
the sweetness and high nutritional
value of the newly-forming plant.
Malt powder for use in malted milk
is readily available on the market
and is commonly sold as a bedtime
drink which is usually taken hot.
Some powders need to be added to
milk but most contain a skim milk
powder and are reconstituted in
water—this type is surprisingly low
in fat. Either will work well,
although the latter adds a luscious
creamy richness to the shake. To
make a maltie, simply sprinkle the
powder into the blender where it
will dissolve during the blending
process. Malt powder can also be
added to any of the recipes given in
the section on chocolate shakes
(see pages 29 to 32).

Malted *Vanilla Shake*

A simple, yet satisfying shake.

1 cup cold whole milk
1 Tbsp. malt powder
2 scoops good vanilla ice cream
Sugar or honey (optional)
Chocolate powder or ground
   cinnamon, to decorate

Combine the milk, malt powder,
and vanilla ice cream in the blender
and process until smooth. Taste
and add sugar or honey to sweeten
as desired. Pour over ice and
sprinkle over a little chocolate
powder or ground cinnamon
to decorate.

Variation
Malted Chocolate Shake: To
make a delicious chocolate shake
substitute chocolate ice cream in
the above recipe. You can also use
chocolate milk or enhance the
chocolate flavor by adding
chocolate syrup.

Chocolate Shakes

Few people can resist a large glass of iced, liquid chocolate topped with even more chocolate or other sweet temptations. The richness and taste of the shake really does depend on the type of ice cream that you use. The rich dark Belgium-style chocolate ice cream is undoubtedly for serious chocoholics; others prefer a slightly less cloying, lighter-textured ice cream.

Here are two different methods of making chocolate milk shake: one uses chocolate ice cream; the other chocolate milk. There are various other methods mentioned in this book. See Chocolate Truffle page 34, and Malted Chocolate Shake, page 28.

Chocolate *Shake*

Simple, rich, delicious, this is the basic, but ultimate chocolate shake.

1 cup whole milk
1 scoop chocolate ice cream

Place the milk and the ice cream in the blender and process until smooth. Pour into a glass and top with one of the options given below.

Variations:
You can select the chocolate ice cream of your choice; Belgian chocolate, rich chocolate, malted chocolate …

Chocolate Shake Variations:
The Chocolate Shake is delicious, but if you want a change you can try any of these variations:

Chocolate Chip: Stir 2 tablespoons semisweet chocolate chunks or chips in by hand. Add white chocolate chips for a change.

Adult Chocolate Chip: As above, but also add 2 tablespoons brandy, Cointreau, crème de caçoa, Amaretto, or Irish Cream.

After Dinner Chocolate: Stir 2 to 3 crushed after dinner mints depending on size in by hand—the ones with the crunchy minty bits are best.

Creamy Chocolate: Substitute up to ½ cup half and half for the milk.

Chocolate Cookie: Stir 1 large or 2 to 3 small cookies into the shake by hand. Remember to drink this one quickly or the crunch will be gone from the cookies. Try chocolate chip, chocolate mint cookies, or chocolate orange cookies.

Chocolate Peanut Butter: Add up to 4 tablespoons crunchy peanut butter with the ice cream.

Rocky Road: Add 2 tablespoons mini marshmallows and 2 tablespoons mixed chopped nuts, and top with more of the same.

Chocolate Almond: Add up to 1 tablespoon almond syrup or a few drops of natural almond extract.

Chocolate Banana: Add 1 small banana with the chocolate ice cream and milk.

Neapolitan: Stir ¼ cup chopped fresh strawberries into the shake by hand. Top with strawberry sauce and toasted coconut. Other fruits, such as raspberries and peaches, are good too.

Chocolate Praline: Add 3 tablespoons crushed praline. Top with an extra spoonful.

Toppings
Top your basic chocolate shake with any of the following ingredients used alone or in combination:

★ *Whipped cream.*
★ *An extra scoop of ice cream: try vanilla, white chocolate, or egg-nog for extra creaminess; raspberry for a Neapolitan-style shake; macadamia, pecan, or almond for a nutty crunch; chocolate chip for a chocolate crunch.*
★ *Sauces: chocolate, strawberry, fudge, or butterscotch sauce— these are really good over an extra scoop of ice cream.*
★ *Chocolate powder.*

★ *Liqueurs are good over extra ice cream—choose a simple, untextured chocolate or vanilla ice cream.*
★ *Chocolate chips and candies.*
★ *Grape nuts.*

★ *Syrups are best poured over extra ice cream. Try some of the more unusual ones such as toasted marshmallow or an alcoholic flavoring (without the alcohol) such as rum or Irish Cream.*
★ *Spices: Try cinnamon, nutmeg, or apple pie spices.*
★ *Nuts such as toasted pecan, almond, macadamia, or filbert.*
★ *Vermicelli.*

Candy *Bar*

Candy bar ice creams are very popular. The ones that are prepared in an ice cream parlor can be used in shakes but those that are individually wrapped and sold in the market do not make successful shakes. Try this home-made version. It does not contain a candy bar, but it has all their indulgent ingredients.

½ cup whole milk
1 scoop rich chocolate ice cream
1 scoop vanilla ice cream
1 Tbsp. butterscotch sauce
2 Tbsp. semisweet chocolate
   chips

TOPPING
1 scoop vanilla ice cream
Butterscotch sauce
Chopped, toasted unsalted
   peanuts or almonds

Blend together the milk, chocolate and vanilla ice creams, and butterscotch sauce. Pour into a glass, then stir in the chocolate chips by hand. Top with more vanilla ice cream and drizzle over plenty of butterscotch sauce. Sprinkle with the chopped nuts. You can go a step further and decorate the glass with a caramel star.

Mocha *Shake*

This is always a popular choice and the coffee tempers the sweetness of the chocolate. There are two ways of making this recipe: one uses coffee ice cream; another has coffee flavoring

¾ cup whole milk
¼ cup strong black or espresso
   coffee
2 scoops chocolate ice cream
Whipped cream, chocolate-coated
   coffee beans, or grated
   chocolate, to decorate
or
1 cup chocolate milk
2 scoops coffee ice cream
Whipped cream, chocolate-coated
   coffee beans, or grated
   chocolate, to decorate

Place all the ingredients in a blender and process until smooth. Top with whipped cream and garnish with chocolate-coated coffee beans or grated chocolate.

If you are using ice cream, add around half a scoop of coffee ice cream with the chocolate.

Alternatively, blend in 1 teaspoon of good quality freeze-dried coffee or 1 tablespoon coffee syrup, remembering that the latter will also add sweetness. To use fresh coffee, add about ¼ cup chilled, strong black coffee and reduce the milk to ¾ cup. Add a dash of half and half for extra creaminess.

Double *Chocolate Shake*

Chocolate milk can be purchased or made at home from a chocolate syrup which can be mixed cold. Hot milk drinks form a skin and tend to come out of the solution when chilled. Cover with plastic wrap to prevent a skin from forming and stir well before adding to the blender.

1 cup chocolate milk
2 scoops chocolate ice cream

Place the milk and the ice cream in the blender and process until smooth. Pour into a glass and top with one of the options.

Variations
Triple Chocolate: Add an extra tablespoon cocoa powder.

Flavored Chocolate: Use a flavored chocolate drink such as chocolate orange.

Honest *Coffee Shake*

This is a basic coffee shake, but it is simply delicious.

**1 cup strong coffee (instant or
 ground), chilled**
**½ cup whole milk or half
 and half**
1 scoop coffee ice cream
Ice
½ to 2 tsp coffee syrup

TOPPING
Whipped cream (optional)

Place the coffee, milk or cream, and
ice cream in the blender along with
ice, if your blender can take it.
Process until smooth. Pour into a
glass with a little more ice and
sweeten to taste with the coffee
syrup. Top with whipped cream,
if desired.

Coffee Shakes

There is nothing nicer than a good
iced coffee on a summer's day,
except for a great coffee shake.
There are several ideas in this
section using various types of
coffee, rich Italian espresso for the
serious coffee drinker, flavored
coffees for the more playful, and
regular coffee for everyday use.

Tip

*The amount of sugar added to
a coffee shake is an individual
matter. Even people who take
their hot coffee without sugar
will find that the flavor of a
shake is improved with a little
sugar or better still, coffee syrup.
The sugar needs to be added to
the blender and the syrup can
be added afterwards, drop by
drop, until it is just right.*

1. Make a coffee syrup by
adding 6 scoops of coffee to 1
cup of boiling water. Infuse for
10 minutes, then strain. This
will make about ¾ cup coffee.
Add ¾ cup sugar and heat
gently until dissolved. This
syrup is too sweet to form the
basis for a coffee shake but is
the best sweetener. **2.** Place in
a sterilized bottle and it will
keep for one month in the
refrigerator.

Espresso *Freddo*

This is a strong, full-flavored coffee shake—quite the best if you crave real coffee. A topping of whipped cream adds delicious richness, but the coffee addict may prefer it solo.

½ cup Italian espresso coffee, chilled
½ cup whole milk
1 scoop vanilla ice cream
½ to 2 tsp. coffee syrup

TOPPING
Whipped cream (optional)

Chocolate-coated espresso coffee beans
Amaretti cookie, to serve

Place the espresso coffee, milk, and vanilla ice cream in a blender and process until smooth. Pour into a glass (with a saucer), over ice cubes. Sweeten with the coffee syrup. Top, if desired, with whipped cream decorated with chocolate-coated espresso coffee beans. To serve this shake in true Italian style, place the amaretti cookie on the side of the saucer.

Frappuccino
Make the Espresso Freddo as above adding ½ scoop chocolate ice cream to the blender. Top with whipped cream sprinkled with powdered chocolate or cinnamon.

Spiced *Coffee*

If desired, use a brandy or liqueur-flavored coffee. Alternatively, add 1 to 2 tablespoons brandy or coffee liqueur to the cooled coffee prior to adding the ice cream. For a cream liqueur or creamy coffee effect, use vanilla ice cream; for a rich, dark coffee, select coffee ice cream.

1 cup fresh, strong black coffee
½ to 2 tsp. sugar
2 whole allspice berries
2 whole cloves
One 1½-inch piece of cinnamon
2 scoops vanilla or coffee ice cream

TOPPING
Whipped cream
Cinnamon stick (if liked)

Place the hot coffee in a jug with the sugar and spices. Let cool. Strain and chill. Place the coffee in the blender with the ice cream and process until smooth. Serve with fresh whipped cream, topped with a cinnamon stick, if desired.

Chocolate *Truffle*

The chocolate complements the coffee flavor very well.

1 cup strong chocolate truffle coffee, chilled
½ cup whole milk
1 scoop vanilla ice cream
½ to 2 tsp. coffee syrup or sugar
Ice

TOPPING
Whipped cream
Grated chocolate

Place the coffee, milk, and ice cream in the blender and process until smooth. Pour into a glass with a little ice and sweeten to taste with the coffee syrup. Top with a swirl of whipped cream and garnish.

Minty
Orange Coffee

This shake has a fragrant, refreshing taste and is a good "pick-me-up" brunch shake. Prepare the coffee the day before, cover, and leave in the refrigerator overnight.

1 cup orange-flavored coffee
1 sprig of fresh mint
1 thin piece of orange peel (about
½ × 3 inches), pith removed
1 scoop coffee ice cream
Small piece orange peel
(optional), to decorate

Pour the coffee over the mint and orange peel. Leave until cold. Cover and refrigerate. Place the coffee and the ice cream in the blender and process until smooth. Float a couple of pieces of fresh orange peel on the top of the coffee.

Tip
In the days of the soda fountain, a shake would always be accompanied by a glass of iced water.

Syrup-based Shakes

The range of syrup flavors now available allows for an infinite variety of syrup-based shakes to be made at home. However, these shakes are for those with a sweet tooth. The combination of sugar in the ice cream and sugar in the syrup makes them very sweet indeed. Bear this in mind when making these drinks. If you are making ice cream at home, reduce the sugar content by up to one quarter.

Cherry *Treat*

A basic milk-based shake.

2 Tbsp. cherry-flavored syrup
1 Tbsp. vanilla-flavored syrup
1 cup ice cold whole milk
Lemon juice, to taste

TOPPING
Scoop of vanilla ice cream
 (optional), ground cinnamon,
 and a cherry

Stir the flavored syrups into the cold milk, try a little, and then add lemon juice to taste. Serve over ice cubes. Top with a scoop of ice cream, if using. Sprinkle a little cinnamon on top and decorate with a fresh cherry.

Above: **Cherry Treat**

Creamy *Cherry*

A basic ice cream-based shake.

2 Tbsp. cherry-flavored syrup
1 Tbsp. vanilla-flavored syrup
½ cup ice cold whole milk
2 scoops of vanilla ice cream
Lemon juice, to taste

TOPPING
Whipped cream or ice cream
Ground cinnamon

Place all the ingredients except the toppings into the blender and process until smooth. Top with whipped cream or ice cream (if using). Sprinkle a little cinnamon on top.

Preserve-based Shakes

Preserves can be used to produce sweet shakes that are similar to those made with syrups; however, they have more texture. Look out for preserves that are sweetened with natural fruit sugars and those with a reduced sugar content.

PBJ

The classic combination of peanut butter and jelly for the all-American kid.

3 Tbsp. grape jelly
1 cup whole milk
3 scoops ice cream
2 Tbsp. crunchy peanut butter

Place the grape jelly, milk, and ice cream in the blender and blend for 30 seconds. Add the peanut butter and process until evenly mixed. Do not over-blend or the crunch may be lost. Serve in paper cups.

Above: **Blueberry Vanilla**

Blueberry *Vanilla*

The sparkling taste of blueberries contrasts with the smoothness of the vanilla.

3 Tbsp. blueberry preserve
1½ Tbsp. lime juice
1 cup whole milk
3 scoops vanilla ice cream
4 blueberries, lime slice and peel

Place all the ingredients in a blender and process until smooth. Serve in a tall, clear glass decorated with blueberries threaded onto a toothpick, lime slice and zest.

Variations

Use strawberry, pineapple, and apricot preserves, and even bitter marmalade which produces an orange-flavored shake, balanced where the sweetness is cut by the bitterness of the chopped peel.

Canned Fruit Shakes

These shakes taste like a cross between the fresh fruit and the preserve shakes. Use fruits in natural juices where possible as these are less sweet. Soft-fleshed fruits, such as strawberries and raspberries, can be puréed without their juice; firmer fruits, such as apricots and peaches, need about ¼ cup of the preserving liquid to make a smooth purée.

Momma's *Strawberry Shake*

This is a strawberry shake of childhood memories.

½ **can strawberries**
¾ **cup whole milk**
¼ **cup half and half**
2 **scoops vanilla or strawberry ice cream**
Mint leaves (optional), to decorate

Drain the strawberries and place in the blender. Blend until puréed. Add the milk, half and half, and ice cream and process until smooth. Pour over ice cubes. If available, decorate with a sprig of fresh mint.

Peaches *& Cream*

The addition of a peach liqueur gives a little kick to this delightfully refreshing shake.

½ **can peach halves**
½ **cup whole milk**
¼ **cup half and half**
1½ **scoops vanilla ice cream**
3 **Tbsp. peach liqueur**

TOPPING
1 **scoop vanilla or peach ice cream and peach slices**

Purée the peach halves with about ¼ cup juice until smooth. Pour about one-quarter of the purée into a jug and set aside. Add the milk, half and half, 1½ scoops of ice cream, and the peach liqueur. Process until smooth. Pour into the glass and top with the remaining scoop of ice cream. Drizzle the reserved peach purée over the ice cream and decorate the glass with peach slices.

Right: **Peaches & Cream**

Frappés

A frappé is a combination of syrup, ice cream, and ice cubes blended until really smooth, creamy, and frothy. Frappés can only be successfully made in a high-powered, freestanding blender. If you are using the food processor to make your shakes, do not use the blender attachment but make frappés in the regular bowl with the sharp blade. Because of the size of the bowl, it is probably more successful to make double the quantities given. Use 3 large or 4 small ice cubes per drink. A frappé can be topped up with either cold whole milk or club soda. Serve in very thin, tall glasses that have been chilled in the freezer.

Maple Leaf
Frappé

This drink is very refreshing and works well with soda or milk.

2 Tbsp. maple syrup
3 to 4 ice cubes
1 scoop vanilla ice cream
Club soda or whole milk

Place the maple syrup, ice cubes, and ice cream in the blender and process until the ice cubes are incorporated and the mixture is smooth and frothy. Pour into a cold glass and top up with club soda or milk. Stir and serve.

Variations
Chocolate Frappé: Replace the maple syrup with any chocolate syrup—chocolate cinnamon and mocha work well. Top the frappé with whipped cream.

Strawberry *Frappé*

This drink is a great hit in all the restaurants around Hollywood.

6 halved strawberries
1½ to 2 Tbsp. strawberry syrup
½ tsp. lime juice
3 to 4 ice cubes

1 scoop strawberry or vanilla
  ice cream
Club soda
Strawberry slices, orange slices,
  and mint leaves, to decorate

Place the strawberries, strawberry syrup, lime juice, ice cubes, and ice cream in a blender and process until it becomes a creamy froth. Pour into a chilled glass and top up with club soda. Stir and serve decorated with a flourish of fruit slices and mint leaves.

Variation
No-fat Strawberry Frappé: Not quite a proper frappé, but you can use strawberry sherbet or strawberry sorbet in place of the ice cream.

Milk Shakes

There are plenty of excellent milk shake recipes that do not use any ice cream or sorbet at all. Many childhood milk shakes come into this category—remember raspberry milk shakes made from syrup that were drunk on a high stool in the kitchen or at the diner?

Frosted
Summer Fruits

Frozen fruit works really well when combined with milk. It tastes like a smoothie, with all the thickness and richness you would expect. Simple flavors work well too: for instance, strawberries on their own are delicious.

**½ cup mixed frozen summer
   fruits**
1 cup whole milk
**1 to 1½ Tbsp. sugar syrup,
   sugar, or honey**
Fresh lemon balm or mint leaves

Place the fruits straight from the freezer into the blender. Add the milk and sugar syrup, sugar, or honey and process until smooth. Taste and add a little more sugar, if required. Sift into a chilled glass through a non-metallic strainer. Decorate with fresh lemon balm or mint leaves.

Banorange *Cream*

If you can't use half and half in this one, use whole milk and a dash of cream.

1 cup chilled orange juice
1 very small or ½ medium
banana
½ cup half and half
Orange slices, to decorate

Place all the ingredients except the orange slices in the blender and process until smooth. Pour into chilled glasses and decorate with orange slices.

Raspberry *Cheesecake*

The addition of the cottage cheese increases the nutritional value of this shake and adds a slight sharpness to the flavor. Try it with other sweet syrups too, such as strawberry, cherry, or blueberry.

1 cup whole milk
2 Tbsp. cottage cheese
1 to 2 Tbsp. raspberry syrup
Few drops lime juice
Frozen raspberries, to decorate

Blend all the ingredients together until the cottage cheese is smooth. Taste and add more lime juice, if required. Serve in a chilled glass and decorate with a few frozen raspberries.

Fortified Shakes

Although some shakes are undoubtedly bad news for the heart and waistline, they can be of nutritional benefit to fussy children, the sick, and the elderly, providing a good way of sneaking nutritional goodies into the diet. They also make excellent drinks for a high energy start to the day. Malt powder, wheat germ, additional proteins, and calcium in the form of skim milk powder can all be added to a tasty shake. Whole eggs can also be beaten into shakes for added protein, but be sure that uncooked eggs come from a reputable source and do not give these drinks to pregnant women, the very young, or to the ill or elderly. Alternatively, use a pasteurized dried egg powder, made up according to the manufacturer's instructions.

Breakfast
Orange

This recipe makes a great start to the day. Add honey to break the taste buds in more gently, but remember that the frozen yogurt is usually pretty sweet.

1 cup chilled orange juice (fresh if possible)
2 scoops vanilla or orange frozen yogurt or ice cream
1 egg (see note, page 4)
2 tsp. wheat germ
1 Tbsp. honey (optional)
Orange slice, to decorate

Combine all the ingredients in a blender and process until smooth. Pour into a chilled glass decorated with an orange slice and serve with whole wheat raisin muffins.

Serious *Lassie*

This is a shake for the serious enthusiast—it contains honey, a great soother, and brewers' yeast which is exceptionally rich in B-complex vitamins. A great pick-me-up.

1 cup chilled whole milk
¼ cup powdered skim milk
2 tsp. molasses or honey

1 tsp. brewers' yeast
2 scoops vanilla ice cream or frozen yogurt
Raspberries and mint leaves, to decorate

Combine all the ingredients for the shake in a blender and process until smooth and frothy. Serve in a chilled glass. Decorate with a few raspberries and mint leaves.

Variation
Earnest Vegan Shake: Use soy milk and soy dessert ice-cream substitute and omit the powdered skim milk.

Banana *Strawberry Surprise*

The surprise comes from all the goodies slipped into the blender; the creaminess of the banana and strawberries, the tang of lemon frozen yogurt, and the nutty flavor of wheat germ that adds nutrition to the shake. For a change, use orange juice in place of milk.

1 very small banana
6 large strawberries
½ cup whole milk
2 Tbsp. skim milk powder
1 Tbsp. malt powder
2 tsp. wheat germ
2 tsp. raw sugar
2 scoops lemon frozen yogurt
Ground cinnamon

Combine all the ingredients except the frozen yogurt and ground cinnamon in the blender and process until the banana and strawberry is puréed and the sugar dissolved. Add the frozen yogurt and a good shake of cinnamon. Blend until smooth. Serve in a chilled glass.

Variation
High Protein Surprise: Add 1 whole egg (see note, page 4) with the fruit.

Smoothies & Coolers

Using frozen yogurt in place of ice cream when making shakes has become increasingly popular over the last few years. The yogurt has a clean, fresh taste and its texture resembles soft-serve ice cream which means that it combines particularly well with fruit to make delicious iced drinks. Most purchased frozen yogurt has the advantage of being low in calories and although this does mean that stabilizers and emulsifiers have to be used, still there can be no doubt that yogurt is healthier than cream.

Easy Frozen *Yogurt*

This simple frozen yogurt is best made with Russian-style yogurt, which imparts a creamy richness. Mandarin makes a good choice of flavor for a basic yogurt as it blends well with most other fruits and can be substituted in the recipes given over the next few pages.

Frozen Yogurt Smoothies

The following recipes are just a few of the delicious drinks that you can make using frozen yogurt. Use whatever fruit you have to hand and combine it with a store-bought frozen yogurt or one that you have made yourself.

2 tsp. cornstarch
One 15 fl. oz. (¾ pt.) can
   mandarin oranges in their
   natural juices
2 Tbsp. honey
1½ cups yogurt

Blend the cornstarch to a paste with a little of the liquid from the mandarins and pour into the blender along with the remaining contents of the can. Pour over the honey and blend until smooth. Add the yogurt and process just long enough to combine. Transfer to the ice-cream machine and churn until firm. Use immediately or freeze until required. Transfer to the refrigerator for about 15 to 20 minutes before using to allow for easier serving.

Variations

Substitute fresh or canned strawberries, apricots, pineapple, or pitted cherries. Bananas work well too. If using fresh fruit, add ½ cup fruit juice. For a smooth texture, strain the fruit through a non-metallic strainer before combining with the yogurt.

Apricot & Mandarin *Smoothie*

The rich flavor of apricots is stunning, however this basic recipe can be adapted just by changing the fruit.

10 apricots, canned or fresh
1 cup apple juice
2 scoops mandarin or orange
    frozen yogurt
2 to 3 tsp. honey
Toasted almonds, to decorate

Place the apricots in the blender with the juice and blend until smooth. For a smooth smoothie, pass the fresh fruit purée through a non-metallic strainer and return to the blender. Add the frozen yogurt and honey to taste, and process until smooth. Serve over ice, decorated with toasted almonds.

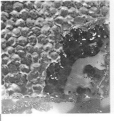

Variations

Nectarine Smoothie: Remove the skin and pit from a very ripe nectarine and substitute for the apricots.

Mango & Papaya Smoothie: Use the flesh from one half of a medium-sized ripe mango and half a small, ripe papaya in place of the apricots. Tropical fruit juice can be substituted for the apple juice.

Cherry Pie *Smoothie*

The almond extract brings out the flavor of the cherries while adding an interesting hint of almonds.

**15 pitted black cherries, either
   very ripe or canned**
¾ cup cranberry juice
2 scoops vanilla frozen yogurt
¼ tsp. almond extract
Fresh cherries, to decorate

Place all the ingredients in a blender and process until smooth. Sift through a non-metallic strainer into an ice-filled glass. Decorate with fresh cherries.

Tip
Place a few berries or small pieces of chopped fruit in the base of the glass. Serve the smoothie with a long-handled spoon so that the goodies at the bottom can all be scooped out.

Frozen *Mint Lassie*

These drinks are popular in India where there are many variations based on fruits, spices, and flower waters. The following is an iced lassie. Vanilla frozen yogurt may be used but for an authentic taste, make your own frozen yogurt omitting all flavorings.

8 fresh mint leaves
½ cup lowfat milk
**2 scoops plain or vanilla
   frozen yogurt**
Sugar, to taste
Mint leaves, to decorate

Place the mint leaves and the milk together in a blender and process until the leaves are finely chopped. Add the frozen yogurt and sugar to taste. (The quantity of sugar will vary depending on the sweetness of the frozen yogurt.) Place in a glass and top up with extra milk, as necessary. Serve over ice, decorated with fresh mint leaves.

Variations
Sparkling Lassie: Substitute club soda for milk.

Rosewater Lassie: Omit the mint and use 1 to 2 teaspoons of rosewater. This drink may be based on milk or club soda.

Fruit Lassie: Make Rosewater Lassie but add ¼ cup chopped fruit to the blender. Use a complementary-flavored fruit plus frozen yogurt in either plain or vanilla flavors.

Right: **Winter Summer Berry Smoothie**

Winter Summer Berry *Smoothie*

This store-cupboard smoothie can remind you of summer all year round.

**3 Tbsp. strawberry ice cream
 topping or preserve**
1 cup summer fruits juice
½ cup frozen mixed summer fruits
2 scoops strawberry frozen yogurt
Few drops natural vanilla extract
Frozen berries, to decorate

Place all the ingredients in the blender and process until smooth. Sift into an ice-filled glass through a non-metallic strainer. Decorate with frozen berries. Use a small bunch of frozen berries, if available.

Variation
Milky Summer Berry Smoothie:
Use only 2 tablespoons of strawberry topping and reduce the mixed summer fruits juice to ½ cup. Add ½ cup whole milk.

Blue Banana *Breakfast*

This is a great treat for children or for someone who is feeling unwell.

1 cup fresh or frozen blueberries
1 banana
1 Tbsp. wheat germ
¼ tsp. lemon juice
2 scoops vanilla frozen yogurt
1 Tbsp. maple syrup
Ground cinnamon, to decorate

Place all the ingredients except the cinnamon in the blender and process until smooth. Pour into the glass and top with a good dusting of cinnamon.

Variation
Simple Banana Breakfast: Omit the blueberries and wheat germ, and substitute honey for the syrup.

Frozen *Apples & Pears*

Apples work better with yogurt than with ice cream. If you make frozen yogurt at home, try using an apple and pear-flavored yogurt as the base. Alternatively, use the recipe given on page 46 omitting the mandarins and substitute 2 ripe pears, peeled and cored, and ¼ cup apple concentrate.

½ cup apple juice
1 large, very ripe pear, peeled
** and cored**
2 scoops vanilla or apple and
** pear frozen yogurt**
¼ tsp. apple pie spices
Apple pie spices, to decorate

Place the apple juice and pear in the blender and process until smooth. Add the frozen yogurt and spices, and process until blended and frothy. Decorate with a light dusting of apple pie spices.

Grapeberry
Smoothie

This smoothie is a wonderful color. You want one even if you are not thirsty.

⅔ cup fresh raspberries
1 cup grape juice
2 scoops raspberry frozen yogurt
2 tsp. sugar syrup or honey
Few drops vanilla extract
Lemon balm leaves, to decorate

Place all the ingredients in the blender and process until smooth. Sift through a non-metallic strainer into an ice-filled glass. Decorate with fresh lemon balm leaves.

Left: **Frozen Apples & Pears**

Sherbet Shakes

Shakes made from sherbet have a light creaminess and a slightly sharp edge to them which is thirst-quenching and flavorful without the overpowering richness of an ice cream-based shake. Sherbets are sometimes made from buttermilk which also has a characteristic acidic taste. In fact, buttermilk can be combined with sherbet to make a lovely refreshing drink that will be enjoyed even by those who protest their dislike of buttermilk.

Simple *Home Made Sherbet*

This is a basic recipe that can be adapted by simply using other flavored juices. Great sherbets can be made from orange, mango, summer fruits, and tropical juices as well as peach and apricot nectar. Buttermilk can be substituted for the milk, if desired, in which case reduce the lemon juice to 1 tablespoon.

½ cup unsweetened pineapple juice
1 tsp. grated lemon peel
⅓ cup lemon juice
½ cup sugar
Pinch salt
2 cups cold whole milk

Combine all the ingredients together in a bowl. The milk may curdle slightly but this is usual and will not be noticeable in the final sherbet. Place in the ice-cream machine and churn for 20 to 25 minutes until stiff. Transfer to a freezer box. Place in the refrigerator for 15 to 20 minutes before using.

Pinemelon
Sherbet Shake

*A very basic sherbet that can be
adapted to include your favorite
fruits and sherbets.*

1 cup pineapple juice
**½ cup diced Chanterelle or
    Cantaloupe melon**
**2 scoops pineapple–lemon
    sherbet**
Crushed ice
Maraschino cherry, to decorate

Combine the pineapple juice,
melon, and sherbet in the blender
and process until smooth. Pour
over crushed ice and serve with
a maraschino cherry.

Caribbean
Sherbet

A tropical treat—if you don't have the coconut milk, just omit it and decorate with toasted coconut instead. The recipe calls for pineapple–lemon sherbet, but orange, lemon, or even mango could be substituted. Add a few chunks of pineapple with the mango to enhance the mixed tropical taste.

**½ diced fresh mango or 3 slices
    canned mango**
1 tsp. coconut milk powder
**¾ cup orange and passion fruit
    juice**
**2 scoops of pineapple–lemon
    sherbet**
**Toasted coconut or slices of
    tropical fruit, to decorate**

Combine all the ingredients in the blender and process until smooth. Serve over ice, decorated with toasted coconut or slices of tropical fruit.

Variation
Caribbean Sherbet Float: Top the Caribbean Sherbet with another scoop of sherbet and decorate with passion fruit pulp.

Above: **Caribbean Sherbet**

Orange *Tang*

The fruity flavor of the orange juice blends well with the buttermilk and you really cannot tell that there is any buttermilk there. This drink makes a nice nutritious treat for a child who is not feeling well.

**Half 6 oz. can frozen orange juice
    concentrate, slightly defrosted**
1 cup chilled buttermilk
1 tsp. honey
2 tsp. wheat germ (optional)
**2 scoops orange, or
    pineapple–lemon sherbet**
Orange slices, to decorate

Process all the ingredients together in a blender until smooth and frothy. Pour into an ice-filled glass. Decorate with orange slices.

Sorbet Coolers

There is nothing more perfectly thirst quenching than a cooler on a hot summer day. They are full of fruity flavor and vitamins and being fat-free, coolers can be enjoyed without concern. Reduced and sugar-free sorbets are available too. Just about any kind of fruit works in these drinks, from the humble to the most exotic. Sorbets are available in a wide range of flavors and, if you make your own, then you are spoilt for choice.

Most of the ideas here are based on simple citrus-based sorbets that are available everywhere.

Home Made *Citrus Sorbet*

This fresh fruit sorbet is easy to make and exploits the amazingly tangy flavor of citrus fruits—orange, lemon, and lime to great effect. It is a wonderful base for any refreshing cooler. Including the egg white is optional (see note, page 4) however it does make for a lighter sorbet.

2 cups boiling water
1¼ cups sugar
½ cup freshly squeezed orange juice
½ cup freshly squeezed lemon juice
¼ cup freshly squeezed lime juice
Grated zest of 1 orange and 1 lemon
1 egg white (optional, see note, page 4)

Pour the boiling water over the sugar and stir until dissolved. Cool and chill. Stir in the orange, lemon, and lime juice, along with the grated zest. For a lighter sorbet, beat the egg white until stiff and gradually mix into the citrus mixture. Pour the mixture into the ice-cream machine and churn for about 25 minutes until firm. Transfer to a container and freeze.

Tip
Dried egg white powder made up according to the manufacturer's instructions can be used as a risk-free substitute for fresh egg white.

Waterkey
Cooler

This subtle cooler is for summertime and needs no additional fruit juice other than that from the watermelon.

2 kiwi fruits, peeled
2 cups diced watermelon
2 scoops lemon sorbet
Sugar syrup or honey (optional)
Kiwi slices, to decorate

Place the kiwi fruits, watermelon, and sorbet in the blender and process together until smooth. Pass through a non-metallic strainer to remove stray seeds. Taste and add sugar syrup or honey, as required. Pour over ice and serve decorated with slices of kiwi.

Cranberry–
Orange *Cooler*

A basic, but fantastic cooler—just admire that color!

1 cup cranberry juice
2 scoops orange sorbet
2 to 4 tsp. sugar syrup or honey
Crushed ice
Orange slices, to decorate

Place the cranberry juice, orange sorbet, and 2 teaspoons sugar syrup or honey in the blender and process until smooth. Taste for sweetness and add more sugar syrup or honey, if desired. Pour over crushed ice into a glass and decorate with orange slices.

Variations
Melonberry Cooler: Use melonberry juice in place of cranberry. Add ½ cup diced melon too.

Tropical Cooler: Substitute tropical fruit juice for cranberry. Add ½ cup of diced tropical fruits such as mango, granadilla, or papaya too.

Tip
Make ice cubes from frozen orange or other fruit juice. They won't dilute your drinks as they melt.

Berry *Cooler*

Everyone loves sumptuous summer berries and here their sparkling taste is captured perfectly.

½ cup raspberries
½ cup strawberries
½ cup blueberries
½ cup summer berry juice
2 scoops raspberry sorbet
2 to 4 tsp. sugar syrup or honey
Fresh berries, to decorate

Place the berries, juice, sorbet, and 2 teaspoons sugar syrup or honey in the blender and process until smooth. Taste and add extra sugar syrup or honey, as required. Sift into ice-filled glasses through a non-metallic strainer. Serve decorated with fresh berries.

Above: **Berry Cooler**

Dried *Apricot*

Dried apricots have a more intense flavor than their fresh counterparts and make excellent flavorsome drinks.

10 dried apricots
2 Tbsp. sugar syrup
2 scoops orange sorbet
1 cup orange, peach, and apricot (or similar) juice

Cook the apricots in a little water and cool. Place in a blender with the sugar syrup and 3 tablespoons of the cooking liquor. Blend. Add the sorbet and fruit juice, and whizz until smooth. Strain before serving.

Lemon Tea
Coolie

Iced tea is a popular summertime drink. This version is even cooler. Look out for mint sorbet which can be substituted very successfully for the lemon.

2 cups boiling water
1 tsp. loose tea or 1 tea bag
2 strips lemon zest
2 tsp. sugar
2 Tbsp. lemon juice
4 scoops lemon sorbet
Ice
Lemon zest curls,
** to decorate**

Make the tea by pouring boiling water over the loose tea or tea bag. Add the lemon zest and the sugar, and allow to steep for 15 minutes. Strain (or discard bag), cool, and chill. Mix in the lemon juice and place 1 cup of tea in the blender with the lemon sorbet.

Process and adjust sweetness to taste. Pour over ice and top up with additional tea. Stir and serve decorated with lemon zest curls.

Tip
Any sorbet that has gone icy in the freezer can be used up by making coolers. This is true for ice cream too, so use it for making shakes.

Sodas

In the early days sodas were mostly made from flavored syrup although some were made from fresh fruits or fruit juices. The main criticism of these drinks was that they were too sweet and, to balance the sweetness, a dissolved form of citric acid was added, which the customer could often add to taste. Alternatively, there was a whole range of drinks that used acid phosphate to balance the sugar. Today lemon or lime juice would seem the best substitute. Add this to your drink and serve a wedge of fruit on the side so that the drink can be adjusted to taste.

Syrup Sodas

Sodas based on flavored syrups have long been popular in homes and cafés. Syrup sodas were the mainstay of the original soda fountain – in their heyday a huge variety of syrups were used, but in recent years they have been available in a limited range of flavors – raspberry, strawberry, banana, and chocolate. However, recently the range of flavors available has exploded – almost anything goes!

Cherry Lime *Bitters*

Angostura bitters add a spicy zing to this drink.

Crushed ice
1 Tbsp. cherry syrup
1 Tbsp. lime syrup
2–3 dashes angostura bitters
Club soda
Lime slices, to decorate

Half-fill a tumbler with crushed ice. Pour over the cherry and lime syrup and the angostura bitters. Fill the tumbler with soda and serve decorated with a slice of lime.

Pineapple *Mint Ricky*

This favorite recipe from the 1930s is a lively, refreshing drink.

1½ Tbsp. pineapple syrup
½ Tbsp. mint or crème de menthe syrup (alternatively use a few drops peppermint extract)
Juice of 1 lime
Crushed ice
Club soda
Orange slice, to decorate

Place the syrups in the base of a tall glass and add the lime juice. Stir and add enough crushed ice to half-fill the glass. Pour over the club soda and serve decorated with the orange slice.

Variation
Orange Mint Ricky: Use orange syrup and (preferably) crème de menthe syrup.

Raspberry *Soda*

The vinegar in this recipe is there to offset the sweetness of the syrup.

Crushed ice
2 Tbsp. raspberry syrup
Juice of ½ lemon
Few drops raspberry vinegar
Club soda

TOPPING
1 to 2 Tbsp. raspberries, mashed

Half-fill a tall tumbler with crushed ice. Pour over the syrup, lemon juice, and raspberry vinegar. Add sufficient soda to four-fifths fill the glass and float a little more ice on top. Carefully spoon the mashed raspberries on the ice.

Strawberry *Lemonade*

Although this is a wonderfully sparkling drink, it works with still water too. The secret is in the crushed ice.

3 Tbsp. strawberry syrup
Juice of 1 lemon
Crushed ice
Club soda or still mineral water
Lemon and strawberry slices, to decorate

Place the syrup and lemon juice in the bottom of a tall glass. Fill the glass two-thirds with crushed ice and pour over the soda or mineral water. Decorate with lemon and strawberry slices.

Variations
Pineapple Lemonade: Use pineapple syrup.

Left: **Raspberry Soda**

Fruit Juice Sodas

Fruit juice sodas are similar to the syrup sodas except that they are based on fruit juices. These drinks are delicious, using tangy juices such as cranberry, peach, or apricot nectar and they work equally well with mixed juices such as orange and passion fruit. These are perfect for those who do not like their drinks too sweet. The lower-fat version using sherbet instead of ice cream and a fat-free variation with sorbet in place of the ice cream and cream, both make brilliantly refreshing drinks.

Cranberry *Soda*

For a less creamy soda, omit the cream. Try using cranberry ice cream if it is available.

1 Tbsp. heavy cream
⅔ cup cranberry juice
Club soda
2 scoops vanilla ice cream

Place the cream in a tall glass and add the juice. Stir and add sufficient club soda to three-quarters fill the glass. Add the ice cream, then top up with more club soda.

Variations
Cranberry Cooler: Substitute orange sherbet for the ice cream.

Grape Soda: Use grape juice in place of the cranberry and add 1 teaspoon of lemon juice. Grape sherbet or ice cream must be used or the taste of the grape will be overwhelmed by the vanilla.

Ice Cream Sodas

Ice cream sodas first became the craze more than a century ago. The combination of rich ice cream and sparkling club soda made a refreshing drink which was exotic to look at and fun to consume. Not a lot has changed since those days except that the variety of syrups has changed and the choice of ice cream multiplied. If you are using well-flavored ice cream, add the syrup at your discretion. In any case, avoid using more than 1 to 2 tablespoons of syrup or the drink will be too sweet.

Serve the soda in a glass (ideally a sixteen-ounce one) as the drink creates lots of bubbly foam. A tall spoon is useful as a mixer and to pick off pieces of ice cream from within the drink.

American *Cream Soda*

This soda has a creamy texture and a heady scent of vanilla. As vanilla extract varies in density of flavor, you may need to increase the amount given.

1½ Tbsp. heavy cream
1 to 2 tsp. sugar or corn syrup
¼ tsp. vanilla extract
Club soda
2 scoops vanilla ice cream

TOPPING
Whipped cream (optional)
Maraschino cherries

Place the heavy cream, sugar syrup, and vanilla extract in the bottom of a tall soda glass. Fill the glass three-quarters full with club soda and stir. Add the ice cream and top up with more club soda. Top with whipped cream (if using) and decorate with a maraschino cherry.

Fruit *Soda*

*A similar drink to American Cream
Soda that is based on canned fruit.*

**2 Tbsp. fruit in syrup, such as
    peaches, apricots, or cherries**
Club soda
1 to 2 Tbsp. heavy cream
1 to 2 tsp. sugar or corn syrup
¼ tsp vanilla extract
**2 scoops vanilla ice cream (or a
    complementary-flavored
    ice cream)**
Whipped cream (optional)
Maraschino cherry, to decorate

Chop the fruit into small pieces.
Place in the base of the soda glass
with a little of the syrup. Add the
heavy cream, sugar syrup, and
vanilla extract. Fill the glass three-
quarters full with club soda and
stir. Add the ice cream and top up
the glass with more club soda. Top
with whipped cream and a
maraschino cherry. Serve as for
American Cream Soda.

Variations
Peach Melba: Combine peach
pieces with raspberry ice cream.

Tropsicle: Use crushed pineapple
in syrup combined with 1
tablespoon of coconut milk powder.
Add one scoop of mango ice cream
and one of vanilla.

Raspberry *Cream*

*A slightly simplified and updated version of the ice cream fountain soda.
The intense flavor and color of the raspberries make this soda great to
drink and great to serve at a party.*

**2 scoops well-flavored raspberry
    ice cream**
**1 Tbsp. raspberry syrup
    (optional)**
Club soda

Place one scoop of ice cream in the
glass with the raspberry syrup (if
using). Fill the glass three-quarters
full with club soda. Add the second
scoop of ice cream and top up the
glass with more club soda.

Variations
Creamsicle: Use orange-flavored
syrup in place of sugar syrup, and
orange flavored ice cream.

Bluesicle: Try blueberry ice cream
and use only about 1 teaspoon of
blueberry syrup as both of these
ingredients are very sweet.

Coffsicle: Use coffee ice cream and
coffee, vanilla, sugar, or cane syrup.

Milksicle: Add ¼ cup of whole milk
or 2 tablespoons of heavy cream to
any of the above ideas.

Maraschino Magic: Mix together
½ cup chopped maraschino cherries
and syrup with 2 tablespoons heavy
cream and finish with 2 scoops of
cherry ice cream.

Right: **Maraschino Magic**

New York *Egg Cream*

The original recipe for this called for whipped egg white which today is often omitted. Try the original which is light and fluffy. Alternatively, use pasteurized powdered egg white made up according to the manufacturer's instructions.

2 to 3 Tbsp. chocolate syrup
2 Tbsp. whipped egg white
  (optional, see note, page 4)
½ cup cold whole milk or half
  and half
Club soda

Place the chocolate syrup and egg white (if using) in the base of a tall glass and beat using a fork. Gradually add the milk or cream, blending together with the fork. Top up the glass with club soda and stir.

Variations
Sinful Egg Cream: As above, but top with whipped cream and chipped chocolate pieces.

Banana Egg Cream: Place the chocolate syrup, egg white (if using), and milk or cream in a blender with half a banana. Process until smooth. Pour into the glass and top with club soda.

Old-Fashioned Chocolate *Soda*

Chocolate, chocolate, chocolate—this is maybe the best known and loved soda.

1 to 2 Tbsp. chocolate syrup
1 Tbsp. ice cream or heavy
  cream, whipped
Club soda
2 scoops chocolate ice cream

TOPPING
Whipped cream
Grated chocolate

Place the chocolate syrup in the bottom of a tall soda glass, then add the tablespoon of ice cream or heavy cream. Fill the glass three-quarters full with club soda and stir. Add the ice cream and top up the glass with more club soda.

Top with whipped cream and grated chocolate. Serve with a long-handled spoon and a straw.

Variations
Chocolate Almond Soda: Add 1 tablespoon of almond syrup.

Chocolate Malt Soda: Substitute chocolate malt syrup for the simple chocolate syrup.

Soft Drink Sodas

Originally ice cream sodas were made from club soda, this being the only available form of fizzy drink. However, at the end of the eighteenth century cola syrups became available and the soft drink world was revolutionized. The Brown Cow—an ice cream soda using cola—was born. Today there are all kinds of carbonated soft drinks which can be made into interesting drinks when mixed with ice creams, frozen yogurts, sherbets, and sorbets. The following recipes provide a few ideas but experiment with your own favorites.

Tip

It is important to rest the ice cream in the refrigerator for 15 to 20 minutes before making any of these drinks or the initial mixing of the syrup, juice, or drink will not include the creaminess of the ice cream. If you don't have time, pop the ice cream in the microwave for a few seconds to melt slightly.

Brown *Cow*

This old recipe has never lost its appeal.

1 Tbsp. chocolate syrup
2 scoops vanilla ice cream
Cola

TOPPING
Whipped cream
Maraschino cherry (optional)

Place the syrup and one scoop of ice cream in the bottom of a tall glass with a little cola. Stir and add sufficient cola to three-quarters fill the glass. Add the second scoop of ice cream, then top up the glass with more cola. Top with whipped cream and finish with a cherry.

Variation
Black Cow: Substitute root beer for the cola.

Tropical *Cooler*

A real treat on a scorching day that is ready in a flash.

½ cup tropical fruit juice
2 scoops citrus sorbet
Tropical soda
Pineapple wedge, to decorate

Place the fruit juice and one scoop of sorbet in the blender and process until smooth. Pour into a tall glass and add sufficient tropical soda to three-quarters fill the glass. Add the second scoop of sorbet and top up with more drink. Serve decorated with a pineapple wedge.

Apricot *Nectale*

This recipe is made with apricot nectar but any other dense fruit juice could be used. If ginger ale is not to your taste, then use a lemon–lime soda.

½ cup apricot nectar
2 scoops vanilla ice cream
Ginger ale

Place the apricot nectar and one scoop of vanilla ice cream in the bottom of a tall glass and stir. Add sufficient ginger ale to three-quarters fill the glass. Add the second scoop of ice cream, then top up the glass with more ginger ale.

Ginger *Scream*

This soda is based on ginger ale, with a hint of spice that goes well with orange.

1 Tbsp. heavy cream
1 scoop vanilla ice cream
Ginger ale
1 scoop orange sherbet or sorbet
Orange slices, to decorate

Place the cream and vanilla ice cream in the bottom of a tall glass with a little ginger ale. Stir and add sufficient ginger ale to three-quarters fill the glass. Add the scoop of orange sherbet or sorbet, then top up the glass with more ginger ale. Decorate with a slice of orange.

Tip
An ice cream soda becomes a cooler when it uses sherbet or sorbet.

Pineapple *Cooler*

This drink couldn't be simpler, yet it is one of the most successful recipes.

2 scoops pineapple sherbet
Lemon–lime soda
Slice of pineapple and pineapple
   leaves, to decorate

Place one scoop of pineapple sherbet in the bottom of a tall glass with a little lemon–lime soda and stir. Add sufficient drink to three-quarters fill the glass. Add the second scoop of pineapple sherbet, top up the glass with more drink and decorate.

Variations
Pineapple Iced Soda: Use pineapple sorbet in place of sherbet.

Pineapple Whizz: Place the sherbet (or sorbet) in the blender with about ½ cup of the lemon–lime soda. Process until smooth. Pour into a tall glass and top with additional drink, then stir to mix.

Citrus Whizz: As for Pineapple Whizz, but use citrus sorbet instead of pineapple.

Orange *Cooler*

This recipe has a delicious tang to it. Make it up with ginger ale for a spicy bite, with a good orange soda (preferably one made from real oranges not the sugary, synthetic version) or even with orange-flavored mineral water. Try the grenadine variation for its wonderful color, if nothing else.

1 Tbsp. frozen orange juice concentrate, partly defrosted
1 scoop orange sherbet or sorbet
Ginger ale or orange-flavored soda or mineral water

1 scoop vanilla ice cream
Orange slices, orange zest, and maraschino cherries, to decorate

Place the orange concentrate, sherbet, and about ½ cup ginger ale or orange-flavored soda in the blender and process until smooth. Pour into a tall glass and three-quarters fill with your chosen drink. Add the scoop of vanilla ice cream and top up the glass with more drink. Serve decorated with an orange slice, orange zest, and maraschino cherries skewered on a toothpick.

Variation
Grenadine Orange Cooler: Add 1 to 2 tablespoons of grenadine to the blender and continue as above, or drizzle the grenadine through the finished drink.

Floats

The difference between a float and a soda is that there is no initial mixing of the syrup or ice cream and there is no added cream beyond that in the ice cream. Simply pour the carbonated drink into the glass, add the ice cream or sorbet, and top up with more drink. What could be simpler or more refreshing?

Below: **Strawberry Float**

Root Beer *Float*

Another drink that unites all memories of growing up.

Ice cubes
Root beer, chilled
1 or 2 scoops ice cream

Place a few ice cubes in the bottom of a tall glass and three-quarters fill with root beer. Top with ice cream and serve with a straw.

Strawberry *Float*

This recipe is made using real fruit pieces. There is an exciting range of alcohol-free soft drinks with sophisticated flavors that are based on spices and extracts of tropical fruits. These all make the drink very up-scale. It's a perfect dessert after a spicy meal.

½ cup fresh strawberries, chopped
¾ cup dinner party soda
2 scoops strawberry sherbet or
**   sorbet**
Strawberry slices and lemon balm
**   leaves, to decorate**

Place the strawberries in the base of the glass. Three-quarters fill a glass with the soda and top with sherbet or sorbet. Finish with strawberries and lemon balm leaves.

Slush

Slushes are like coolers but they are made with uncarbonated water or with milk instead of flavored juices or sodas. They are very straightforward to make but to be sure of a successful slush, it is essential that the water or milk is icy cold. If you drink the water from your faucet, then use it in your slush otherwise use a bottled mineral water. Use whole milk in milk slushes and, if you are feeling particularly indulgent, add a dash of cream. Any well-flavored sorbet or combination of sorbets works well in these drinks.

Peach & Apricot *Cream Slush*

This upmarket slush combines the rich luxuriant flavor of apricots with juicy, refreshing peach, to give a velvety, creamy taste. To ensure that you get your slush to the right consistency, make sure that the water and milk are ice cold and that the ingredients are blended together well.

2 scoops peach sorbet
1 scoop apricot sorbet
½ cup chilled water
½ cup chilled whole milk or half and half
Peach slices, to decorate

Place all the ingredients in a blender and process on a low speed until combined. Serve in a tall glass, decorated with slices of fresh peach.

Simple *Citrus Slush*

This is one of the best poolside drinks ever.

1 scoop lemon sorbet
1 scoop orange sorbet
1 scoop lime sorbet
¾ cup chilled water
Lime slices, to decorate

Place all the ingredients in a blender and process on a low speed until combined. Serve in a tall glass, decorated with slices of fresh lime.

Kiwi &
Raspberry Slush

*The indefinable sweet-tart flavor
of kiwi and the sharp tangy kick of
raspberry combine wonderfully to
make this a drink to wake up all
the senses.*

2 scoops kiwi sorbet
1 scoop raspberry sorbet
½ cup chilled water
Kiwi slices, to decorate

Place all the ingredients in a
blender and process on a low speed
until combined. Serve in a tall
glass, decorated with slices of kiwi.

Frozen Cocktails

Cocktails are always great fun and frozen cocktails are even better. They are perfect for warm evenings when they are sipped as the ice melts. Using sorbet or ice cream doesn't dilute the flavors in the same way as crushed ice. However, ice does melt in the presence of alcohol, so do not use too much or the frozen edge to the drink will be lost.

Frozen Strawberry *Daiquiri*

This delicious, refreshing drink is perfect to serve at a cocktail party as it is simple to make but looks and tastes stunning. Make the drink with a cocktail shaker for added effect and imagine yourself in Acapulco as you sip this ice-cool daiquiri.

**4 to 6 Tbsp. (2 to 3 fl. oz.)
  white rum**
½ tsp. lime juice
1 tsp. orange juice
3 fresh strawberries
2 scoops strawberry sorbet
Ice
**Slices of strawberry and mint
  leaves, to decorate**

Combine the rum, lime juice, orange juice, strawberries, and the strawberry sorbet in the blender and slowly process to mix. Alternatively, shake the ingredients together thoroughly in a cocktail shaker. Pour over ice and serve decorated with slices of fresh strawberry and mint leaves.

Variation
Mango Daiquiri: Substitute fresh mango and mango sorbet for strawberries.

Champagne *Coupé*

A very elegant float with several popular variations. Try pink champagne or dry sparkling wine with vanilla ice cream, or a scoop of strawberry sorbet floating on a lake of chilled white wine.

1 glass champagne
**1 scoop raspberry sherbet or ice
  cream**
Lemon zest twist, to decorate

Serve the champagne in a wide glass and float the sherbet or ice cream on top. Stir once, then decorate with a twist of lemon zest.

Right: **Frozen Strawberry Daiquiri**

Tom *Coolie*

This soda is a frozen Tom Collins, a cocktail said to be named after its creator. Drizzle a little framboise into this one if it is too sharp to the taste.

6 Tbsp. (3 fl. oz.) gin
1 tsp lemon juice
2 scoops lemon sorbet
Ice
Club soda
Slice of lemon and a maraschino
  cherry, to decorate

Combine the gin, lemon juice, and sorbet in a blender and process slowly until smooth. Alternatively, shake together in a cocktail shaker. Pour over ice in a tumbler, top up with club soda, and decorate with a slice of lemon and a cherry.

Zabaglione *Shake*

This shake is almost like a frozen dessert. It is very Italian and very good.

6 Tbsp. (3 fl. oz.) marsala
¼ cup whole milk
2 scoops eggnog ice cream or
  vanilla ice cream
2 egg yolks (optional, see page 4)

Grated chocolate

Blend the ingredients together until smooth. Pour and decorate with chocolate.

Pina *Colada*

This makes a delicious shake with or without the rum. For a bit of fun, you can serve this drink in a small, hollowed-out coconut.

¾ cup crushed pineapple
1 cup whole milk
2 scoops ice cream
2 Tbsp. coconut milk powder
6 Tbsp. (3 fl. oz.) white rum
Ice
Grated nutmeg, to decorate

Combine the crushed pineapple, milk, ice cream, and coconut milk powder in the blender and process until smooth. Add the rum and pulse to mix. Pour over ice and sprinkle with grated nutmeg.

Singapore *Slush*

This delicious slush is based on the classic cocktail, the only problem with this slush is that you can't keep going back for more!

3 Tbsp. (1½ fl. oz.) gin
6 Tbsp. (3 fl. oz.) cherry brandy
Ice
2 scoops lemon sorbet
Club soda
Orange slices and a maraschino
  cherry, to decorate

Place the gin and cherry brandy with two ice cubes in a cocktail shaker and shake well. Pour into a glass. Then place the sorbet and a little soda in a blender and process slowly until smooth. Pour into the glass and stir. Top up with additional soda and decorate.

Left: **Tom Coolie**

Tequila *Sunrise*

In general, orange-based cocktails work as well as frozen drinks. Tequila Sunrise is particularly good, but try the variations or follow the same method for your own personal favorite.

2 scoops orange sorbet
2 Tbsp fresh orange juice
6 Tbsp (6 fl oz) tequila
Ice cubes
2 tsp grenadine
Mini scoops of orange or
**   pomegranate sorbet**
Slice of orange, and maraschino
**   cherry, to decorate**

Combine the orange sorbet and juice with the tequila in the blender and slowly process to mix.

Alternatively, shake together in a cocktail shaker. Place 3 or 4 ice cubes in a tall glass and pour over the sorbet mixture. Slowly pour the grenadine into the glass and allow to settle. Stir once and serve decorated with mini scoops of sorbet, a slice of orange, and a maraschino cherry.

Variations
Orange Cloud: Omit the grenadine and use pernod in place of tequila.

Dreamsicle: Omit the grenadine and use 3 tablespoons (1½ fluid ounces) each of vodka and crème de caçao. Use orange sherbet in place of sorbet.

Creolesicle: Substitute 3 tablespoons (1½ fluid ounces) of Malibu and 2 tablespoons (¾ fluid ounce) of rum for the tequila and stir well after adding the grenadine.

Harvey Wallbanger: Replace the tequila with vodka and the grenadine with Galliano and stir well. Decorate with pineapple, cucumber, and a maraschino cherry on a stick.

Moscow *Dream*

A float based on a Moscow Mule.

6 Tbsp. (3 fl. oz.) vodka
2 Tbsp. lemon juice
Ice cubes
Ginger beer
1 scoop lemon sorbet
Sprig of mint, to decorate

Pour the vodka and lemon juice over ice in a tall glass. Three-quarters fill with ginger beer and add the sorbet. Top up with more ginger beer.

White *Prussian*

A vanilla ice cream-based variation on the classic Russian. Both Tia Maria and crème de caçao are sometimes used to make this drink. Choose your favorite.

1 scoop vanilla ice cream
3 Tbsp. (1½ fl. oz.) vodka
3 Tbsp. (1½ fl. oz.) Tia Maria or
**   crème de caçao**
Ice
Grated nutmeg, to decorate

Place the vanilla ice cream, vodka, and Tia Maria or crème de caçao in a blender and process slowly until smooth and thoroughly blended. Alternatively, shake together in a cocktail shaker. Pour into the glass over ice cubes and sprinkle with grated nutmeg.

Fire & Ice Floats

There are a few hot drinks that can be combined with ice cream to make a hot float. These drinks must be prepared very hot and, once the ice cream is added, they should be served immediately or else the ice cream will simply disappear.

Buttered *Rum*

The basis for this recipe is the butterscotch ice cream and this can be refrozen for a month or kept in the refrigerator for up to a week. Make it in larger quantities if it proves popular.

MAKES EIGHT SERVINGS
1 cup brown sugar
½ cup butter
1 cup vanilla ice cream, slightly softened
3 Tbsp. (1½ fl. oz.) of rum per serving
Boiling water
Nutmeg or ground cinnamon, to decorate

Place the brown sugar and the butter in a saucepan and cook over a low heat until the butter and sugar has melted. Combine the sugar mixture with the ice cream in a mixer or blender and process until smooth. This mixture is then thoroughly cooled and kept in the refrigerator or it may be frozen.

Place 1 scoop of frozen mixture or ¼ cup chilled mixture in a cup with 3 tablespoons (1½ fluid ounces) of rum. Fill with boiling water, stir, and serve sprinkled with grated nutmeg or cinnamon.

Hot Toddy *Cold*

It is hard to know whether to describe this as an ice cream with hot liquor topping or a drink topped with ice cream.

6 Tbsp. (3 fl. oz.) calvados
3 Tbsp. (1½ fl. oz.) apricot brandy
3 mini scoops ice cream

Warm the calvados and apricot brandy over a low heat. Pour into a heatproof glass (a glass espresso coffee cup is ideal) and slip in the ice cream. Serve immediately.

Hot Chocolate
Float

The ultimate comfort drink, it is always a pick-me-up on a cold day.

MAKES 4 SERVINGS

⅓ **cup semisweet chocolate chips**
3 Tbsp. sugar
1¼ cups water
2 cups whole milk
¼ cup light cream
½ tsp. vanilla extract
4 scoops vanilla ice cream
**Chocolate powder or ground
   cinnamon, to decorate**

Place the chocolate chips, sugar, and water in a saucepan and slowly bring to a boil; then boil, stirring constantly for 2 minutes. Stir in the milk, cream, and vanilla and heat through—do not boil. Beat with a wire whisk until frothy, then pour into four warmed mugs.

Carefully place a scoop of ice cream into each mug and sprinkle with chocolate powder or cinnamon. Serve immediately.

Bibliography

Dahl, J. O.
Soda Fountain &
Luncheonette Management.
New York and London:
Harper Brothers, 1930.

Damerow, Gail.
Ice Cream! The Whole
Scoop. Lakewood,
Colorado, USA: Glenbridge
Publishing, 1995.

Feltham, Leonard R. M.
Service for Soda Fountains,
Ice Cream Parlours and
Milk Bars, London:
Heywood, 1936.

Liddell, Caroline and
Weir, Robin.
Ices: The Definitive Guide.
London: Grub Street, 1995.

Index

Index